From
a Strident World
of
Soft Prevailing Things

*Poems About Our Human,
Animal and Vegetal Environment*

ALDYTH M IRVINE-HARRISON

Tellwell Talent
www.tellwell.ca

ISBN
978-0-2288-2378-0 (Paperback)
978-0-2288-2379-7 (eBook)

Table of Contents

Creatrix

PHYSIOGRAPHY

Animal Kind

Human Kind

PROFILE

Aldyth Irvine Harrison was born in Kingston, Jamaica, where she received her secondary education at St Hugh's High School for girls. She studied at Concordia (Sir George Williams) and McGill universities. She taught many levels in the Quebec school system.

It was her choir master, the late Brian Brice, and fellow chorister Dr. Thouria Bensaoula, who encouraged her to publish *Patches in & out Two Centuries* which was published in October 2010 by Éditions du Mécène, Beauceville, Quebec.

Her concerns are about the careless handling of our Earth. The dignity of the Earth's environment must be nurtured, respected and preserved. She enjoys telling stories and travelling to different parts of the world.

She resides in Montreal, Quebec, with her husband Robert and family.

DEDICATION

For those who strive to preserve,
to build and to be kind in our daily routine.
Kindness your twin
Sense of Humour
Fortitude Grace
Shared your witty
hilarious space
In Memory of Joanne Walker Al-Khabyyr 1961-2018

In Memory of Sarala Patel 1945-2018
Many ideas were incubated during games of Rumi-cube and Scrabble

ACKNOWLEDGEMENTS

I am so grateful to Roselyn Small for typing so many poems with speed and accuracy. She has been a keen critic and an excellent friend.

Thank you to my cousin Denise Irvine Robertson who rescued me from a computer headed for retirement.

Thanks to Aolani who guided me through technical adversities and Celestine Segers who designed the enchanting covers for both of my publications.

Aldyth Irvine Harrison

Creatrix

WALK WITH ME

Walk with me in silent
travel around meandering
reactors of nuclear parks

Walk with me under clouds
of pollen perfumed smoke

Walk with me when icy
fingers pierce our polite skin

Walk with me when cups of
warmth dismantle painful whims

Walk with me down corridors
of floral wishes whispered cheer

Walk with me over ranges
throwing kisses to thronged atmosphere

Walk with me help me navigate
an abyss of fantastic change
Walk with me Walk with me Walk with me

JUST STUFF

Lying Down
Looking at things
Realization - Now
This is the Stuff
of us.

BLAME

It is nature we say
Nature is neither
evil nor good Will
sway Responds to desires
acts might love delight

EXCUSES

Whether it is a spear, plane
Floating Noun, bar of gold
So many dialectics
to justify the call for war

CASH

Pretty paper designed

with prominent heads

Coins of lesser metals

weigh down pockets cram

purses Copper discarded

ignored by most but

clairvoyant collectors

Wooed cursed incessantly

revered reviled as

if born in banks with

paper homes in documental

style Virtual finance

fashions new history

all part of chip memory

COMMUNIQUE

Dispatch Hear See Feel
Turn off various screens
Remove plugs that relay
unsettling stories
What happened does not
stay it floats Seeps through
every vomitory place
through bolted doors window
seals We feel singular
news before it peals
Tune communiqué on
When felicitous
tidings flow through screens
contentment looms A
cherished time to change
State For expanding
rooms that give little heed
to what we will not
change or do not need

PROVIDENCIA

First Stop

Cooled cocktails of high

breezes Exhaust of

black clouds roll behind

peaks of flowers large

bright fed by cool mountain

rain by tepid sunlight

In out the mists of

shopping eating crossing

overhead vibrating

bridges of simple design

Evening quiet a

family in pain Grief

no stranger to

any place--even in the

wonderment of a high

oxygen hungry angel

lit city of religious

grace Children lively

nurtured with taste Tomorrow's

lovely invites no haste

Second Stop

Hurried hot resting

hands slapping grabbing

at a whine combing

a soft space to pierce

Such a stop to be

squashed flicked off a scaffold's

edge Scavengers scurry
in open daylight

to dine upon mosquito

delight

Now a sigh fatigue

from hugging a case

of books Immigration

Officers sought me

a status There wasn't

a stamp for a part-time

lecturer on Providencia

Suitcases with me

went to live temporarily

in the womb of a

hotel sans reception

Ride on a scooter

ah cooling was fun

Currents of air fled

through strands of my hair

Hotel fan spun furiously

the other way--sucked hungrily

would not share or cool

a drop of purloined air

A change of room oh!

breathe--showering is a

dripping state Insects

popping in and off

subtle smells from an

executioner's purse

wiped this lot from a

Dengue Fever's course

Exploration

Saturday morning

ninety-five degrees

or more A walk around

the Island Marine blue

skies bright orange sun

A cap brushed dark glasses

absorbing perspiration

that sponge the face and

neck with tears of

a spanking hot day

Turned on to a short

road that rallied to

a quay--ended on

a court of sorts or

baseball diamond--place

for many sports A

sunny Hello checked

my thoughts A bearded

man with a talking

stomach that told many

tales of food confirmed

my identity Teacher

walking so far--shock

it is hot He spoke

of friends wondered if

I had been acquainted

People from your country

he chirped--you know Ida

and Rupert and . . . It

has been a long time

my ability to recall

fades in hot summer glare

They were guests dishonoured

departure would be ignominious

his wife clarified all

incensed man cheated

out of land--empty

threats Alcalde used

position to jail

this farmer The tales

he recited longer

than the seventeen

and a half kilometers

saunter in the afternoon

Islanders were open

people so clear No

design in what they

wanted to say

Spontaneous stories

of motorcyclist who

embraced a tree Looks

vastly altered by

medical miracle

two hundred shiny screws

Mother boasted handsome

change to a once homely

incurious face

A quarter to four

now accustomed to

golden light I arrived

at tiny airport

FIVE STEPS TO LAND THE PLANE

I

There are steps to waking
Flush out of bed will
shock nerves disorient heads
A golden son's fate
confirmed by a bullet
single horror in
one hundred years Grief
then illness shrouded
cause Skies unzipped it
poured Mother setting out
to fly from sobbing
island seeking wellness
under foreign skies

II

Pall of silence on
heavy hot day Mind
clouds descended to
clothe each standing on
a short grass fronted
runway Plane warming
silent farewells Emptied
mother on arm of
daughter-in-law chief
medical practitioner
awake alive where
widowhood took some
minutes respite

III

Well-wishers on tarmac
lent silent support
Crew in cockpit nosed
plane out of port Little
flier supported by
walls of atmosphere brushed
clouds Clawed way towards
slightly darkened sky
Whispered monotone
drowned out chattering
waves tossing shattered
bits of water at a
late morning sky Plane
dipped in courteous salute
Traveller disapproved
pinched skin of armrest
plane responded with a
drop then steady retreat
to calm position
relief for a seat

IV

Father of flying fleet
cooped in place scanned violet
skies rippled seas--covered
a yawn dozed in sleep
Quiet was queen Avid
reader behind pilot's
chair noticed booklet
near landing gear Page
number seven opened
revealed five steps to

land this plane Tome balanced
all in its hands Vehicle
nosed towards tiny
bleached white sand running
to meet silver plane
Travellers slapped into
place perhaps by shock
or mild faint Plane touched
down There are steps to
running eating coping
with grief which passes
somehow like water
losing heat to sweet
call of rushing breeze.

THE DANCE AND THE SONG

The slight of a hand
extended with warmth
A lateral nod -smile
powders the ground for
motion and style
Materials are delicate
Well cut tails launched
in low flight as bodies
swish and sway in soft
blaring whispers of
a Waltz of the day

Songs make slaves of persistent
romance Ageless voices
of all special lands
Strings seem to quiver
at the blaring brass
Music an anatomy
of all that has passed

Notes are people prancing
or strolling through Clefs
Treble Bass collide in tune
dancing on pages
clasped in the timbre
of Musical graces

LITTLE THING

Ever remember
the garbage bin by
our Church near Claremont
Street of terribly blue
hyacinths in spring
An accordion bus
lumbered away on
a fair Friday
just as someone tossed
a freshly rolled slim
at the rim of this
newly vacuumed scrubbed
forest green bin

ON THE VERGE

Move over my friend

as far as you can

You will not topple

into the ditch The land

beside is your private pitch

A simple request

to a warrior

to a grandmother

We need your space so

do cooperate Create

a spanking new one

This ancient space is

filled with seasoned energy

complete with the wisdom

of all--of everyone

OUT OF TOUCH

Boisterous beautiful
crack slap thunder
Dart knifed lightning
spitting splitting shattering
with venomous cries
unleashing tears without
reply Dissolving
earth rocks flushing out
vegetation Animal
kingdom must run from
habitual habitation
There is no grudge but
a cry Some of us
are burning our skies

A TRAFFIC SOLUTION

The idea of Zip Lining
came from a Spider who caught
my notice - It built a web
on the roof of a Spiritual
Centre without the steeples
just an Arch above a veranda
with shelter from quick showers
cooling roasted summer days
It must have scurried up the
stony wall and secreted its
threads in a protected cove
There would be babies but of
this I am not sure - it had
hidden companions I surmised
and food quite divinely stored

11
That Spider knew how to travel
no noisy transport tickets
jostling crowds It just zip lined
down then up - protected from
the Elements by stony
arches of a Church's veranda
unsprayed garden with living
food frolicking way below
I think I know this because
We saw this Arthropod of
the order Araneida
on a hot day zip lining from
a high arch to a green and
flowered woodchipped garden floor

111

In Summer this is what I
want to do - slide from the highest
point on a roof - over the
Saskatoon berry trees to
the soft mulched insect ridden
garden floor Transportation
is complex giant wheeled structures
navigating dark grey roads
Speak with spiders at buildings
One may yet show how to relieve
congestion in the City
in summers with festivals galore
Ribbons of streets with moving
chairs - the air swishing with
Zip lining gear. Spiders calling
Children dear! classes are cancelled
until our air has been cleared

PARKING

A rest in unfamiliar
spots In midst of turmoil
sand dust In heart of
rain flowers trees At
places that we freeze
imagination books
or dreams Parking spot
a quiet part of us

Aldyth M Irvine-Harrison

PASSPORT OFFICE

Ahead chairs hooking arms

congenially dispassionately

Return to infant chair

such years since running

away Felt strangeness

of location in time

listened sought comfort

in language colour tone

that welcomed infant ears

years so many years

before in a far away

plot of a universal

dot lit by stars frequent

moonlight washed by oceans

rinsed by rivers streams lakes

Fresh challenges await

new paths for older years

HOME AGAIN

Tenebrous grey sheets

sheltered noises of
gossiping geese - Their
loud complaints translate
It is wet all is obscure
Then it seemed odd queer
water congregating - it
would appear everywhere

This avenging liquid
creates an expanding
dark monster that eats
grows. It gobbles green
retreats - Big structures
grinds on - Confusion
of sounds desperate calls
to the dissolved ground
Wrecked homes are chasing
their sinking accounts
A sense of hopelessness
Creates new Clouds
anguished calls to the
Governments, Banks, Charities
those with enough or more
who will heed the desperate
human animal cries
to a simply harassed sky

SAFETY PIN

Curled tail flattened head
sides hold tears until
thread appears Kingdoms
host pins that catch rents
wait for healing immeasurable
years Split in a tree
fissure on a plain
weeping musters nature's
pins in silver clusters
to patch hold or keep
close shredded fibres
Clutches of keen pins
attend in the wings

SOUNDS

Sounds have destiny
all share a fate
They will emit silence
at the far end of days

We sit in a Bowl
cushioned from sounds
enveloped by silence
short lived profound

Outside a saltus
bowl peppered by pebbles
The noise resounds like a
Tap dancer's intention

On visits into Space
Are we noisy creatures
Does life feel our approach
then secret itself into a
Melodium of instrumental
sound effects

Defy silence stir the Still
call living noise again to cheer
languages of people's music
their dance - unwrite sadness fear

Happy sounds feed the essence
invites scenes of celebration
Cheerful sounds resonate universally
promotes good health excellent energy

Go to a spot climb as high
as can be - shout messages of
joy to a starved atmosphere
Now sit an relax - for joy
bounces back - whatever we send
We are sure to get back

SLEEP

Calm conservation
comfy seat A chat
accord with semi-colon
in house of hurry scurry
rush Sleep slurs darkness
folds to warm restful
state called old Too soon
time polls rolls over
to sprinting space in
racing blurry days

SPECIAL OLYMPIANS

Flush of sports athletes joy
parents pride struggle sublime
Efforts guided practice fun
Games like rehearsals
but with everyone

Action on Speed pumped
from all parts of frame
primed massaged Friendships
play monumental part

Force that forges passions
to instigate speed strength
inoculates crowd with
excitement remoulded from
empathy into enlightenment

Performance offers love
wisdom dignity Insight
sets our learning on
a path of discerning

Disappointment no issue
participation is the key
All are with friends Smiles
merge into laughter
over and over again

SUCH CROSSING

Mechanical pedestrian
on a blue hot day
wheels of cushioned balloons
bounced across black roadway
with red sidewalks of
imitation clay Cars
were reluctant to
change pace stop let this
insolent cushion
roar across Pride pumped
youngster shot into
middle of a newly
preened crosswalk He blew
his whistle--bellows
from youth shocked haughty
lords in stately sedans

He zapped across Explosive
roar donated smoke dust
measured shock to tranquil
pedestrians walking
common-place city blocks

THOUGHT

Powdery puissant afloat
in watery spheres Adrift
on packed warm cold air
Perpetuates insinuates
itself in quiet corners
on universal platforms
nourishes creation
Borders are elastic
tiny ideas leap are
glued to new planted
feet Body ages
mind matures Thought
grows flows outlives then
recreates its source

ZEST

Infuse a zest for
learning Pack in curiosity
stuff my bowl with painted
thoughts kind words with stories
that zoom right through to
the heart Spirit of
learning never depart

Physiography

ALERT

In little corners
tiny breaks from annual
songs merthless praises
Storm waves pound drown
clean beautiful feet
slam doors on old hopes
open permutations --
avenues in uninspected
rage -- the elements
answer in harmony
with our state -- Untie
suffocating threads
Save lovely accord
with eager elements

CIRCLE

Incessant issues
wasted efforts - blew
up trees burnt violets
that peopled green fields
Shelters vacated
planners presumed that
they had won – Ashes
rot nourished lively
seeking place to revive
their state Shapes of trees
irregular free
Colours of fields orange
magenta puce to
some degree Plant kingdom
immortal reconfigures
reforms from forgotten
state to whatever's

innate – Universal laws
as we discover are
generous to a fault
return us wholeheartedly
whatever we shelled out

CLOUD CLEANING

Volcanic efflorescence
felt all around Sulphuric
odours travel with haste
warns air beyond of ashes
Trapped clouds darkened
moving away must
free itself of grit
poisoned malevolent air

COATED

Dust dust frolicking
rolling under beds
clogs the open doors
Perches on vanities
has passion for floors
dark brown or beige
they camouflage their
beige linen state

New machines are sucking
screens – babies escape
into airborne state
Dust likes carpets hides
quiet sound – dust profound
avoids scrutiny into
dubious background

Dust outside savvy
glib – joins forces with
an ear splitting wind
It brags a power
clouds chokes blocks air spaces
Each particle life
it sinks floats propagates
then grows – Dust the basis
of what we find everywhere
on water in air
under seats of chairs

ESSENCE OF TIME

Time we measure by
some light remover
of sight sound tactility
Dark blots spot wan in
elongated rays
of smoky gold sun

FALLEN TREE

A mighty giant

painful to see

imposing carcass on

a bloody green sea

Surrounded by loud

gnawing sounds They have

cut and deafened dying

titan--home to fat creatures

miniature birds strange

fungi that darkened

core extracted liquids

climbed higher for more

Loss inevitable but triumph

is sure in sprouting

of newborn trees

there will be much more

FIGHTING FLOODS

Rolling waters tossing
ground New cake ingredients
all treasures existing
Homes unravelled by floods
land flowing liquid mud
trees adopt unusual
posture Flowers float
away from hosts
What shape will land take
what will be icing
on new Earth cake

FROST FAIRIES

Wet cool cold clear high
attract frail glass that
cling trust Trees shrubs warmed
by white dust in blue
haze where mist fairies
join hands touching feet
around all shapes of trees
Warmth is removed from
touch of frost that brings
blush and carries glow
White lights glitter wave
as aeroplanes streak past
clouds of crystal glades

II

There are the fairies
we're apt to destroy
by attacking their
homeland decimating
the skies What shows
will we see flying
past in minus degrees
How shall we compare
the warmth of inside
when frost fairies we
find we're compelled
to deride

III

Frost will be petrol
for Maples to flow
Sugar candy mapleing*
takes over from tired
frost in spring If white
sprinkles south Tropics smell
cold as undesired fate
calls supine sun to
keep date prepare for
warm humid rainy state

IV

Give berth to world of
deities sprites be keen
keep winter North South
guard warmth in between
Cold inhabitants play
in brown fields of white
Warmth occupy latitudes
twenty-three and a half
degrees on both sides
*Neologism

HOPE

I am only wind

pouring over flats

through hilly gaps over

watery plains pushing

mists into bulbous

clouds--whipping awnings

whispering in trees

It will be mild I'm

simply a breeze to

banish cold heat

ICE ON TRIAL

There is a stillness
In the roar of Furious
Fifties One radiant phenomena
To see a star cross
blinking above stern
navy black sea Southern
Cross deplores sight of
cracking ice downfall
of tumbling white green
walls Life's hope denied
for ice cannot sing
its cold green cords of
coming Antarctic spring

CONSUMING ICE

Ice is persistent
It is not without style
Bribes the artless air
to pour its moisture
over things caught in stream
or inbetween
Ice marries the trees
with kinder precision
Gives diamond tassles
to decorate all things
before the next influx
of below freezing winds

New Technology is natural
Prodigy of human sense
Goes after flirtatious ice
with noisy passion zest
Driver of a rolling mass
of yellow steel performs
a double grind - He chomped
on a banana as ice he
ground into powdery heaps
Life evolves in bare sunlit
dump

INSTINCTS

Quiet magnificent
Guiding thoughts away
from confrontation
or convenient tool
for shouting rules

IT IS

Earth--every line carved
painted with designs
Spaces filled with hope
grace fear Light shakes
unsure gaze Tread upon
souls with remarkable pose

LIGHT MODE

Transition of change
movement at last for
one jellied in a bed
job neighbourhood or
car that travels an
incessant road back
and forth to the same
familiar start
In travel one needs
to fly not weighed in
lead with darkened dye

MORNING LIGHT

Morning sun climbed out
of powder mist that
canopied ridge in
rest Stole crystal jewels
from tips of trees melted
all to golden green
Millions of years each
warrior carved a passage
through the dark Displayed
special light radiant
muted brilliant or dyed

PALM SONG

Tale
White grey bird flew to
clump of fruited palms
Tail vertical careless
of sky she found a
cache red berries on
swaying palm Beak plucked
She paused on a wire
pivoted head with berry
couched in beak Gesture
of thanks before she
eats There will be meals
for many moments

it seems Little calm
in noisy nest Full
stomach precedes rest
The song of a palm
resides in the seeds
Songs of its heritage
played by the breeze
Sharp spears sprout from soil
trunk joins family when
fronds age brown detach
uncovering anchor
light brown bumpy ground

Becoming
Families chattering
inexorably little ones
call upon the wind
to carry their swishing
sounds Base of fronds new
section of trunk with
quiet holes Babies unkempt
shaggy trunks sheds hides
With each stretch smooth trunk
unhampered catches
up to higher growth

Mother Queen
Queen of palms assembled
in noble lines Soldiers
of times tempering
winds protecting infant
shrubs trees offering hope
such dignity in growth

Traveller's Salvation

Palms fan out
reserves water for thirst
in basins at frond's
feet reposing on
succulent fibrous skin

Comestibles
Brown husk as dry as
February's winter dead
yet Spring hides in wombs
fresh baby greens leaping
out to catch warmth gobble
yellowing gold light
Coconut green what
a future you'll feed
reaching somewhat above
buildings over beaches
over path paved streets

Coconut palm flexible
in wind will secure
her nuts with thick woven
string Each breaks away
mature free rolls inches
from whimpering tree
Thirst hunger are quelled
when hide is ripped Water
pours out but jelly
is glued to woody
brown coat Nuts will travel
to extremes--porous
beaches rolling fields
but reply to warm
earth where minerals
rest Rise feed thirsty
fast growing trees
Other palm nuts with
playful names feed children
in between rigorous games
Not all grace tables

dates candied cousins
of dry sandy spaces
are called to cold hot
wet places feed many
Thank you oasis
Low palms red fruit clustered
in bunches For some
birds a leisurely
lunch Ravenous travellers
are satiated plump
Pay tribute to spritely
saplings that donate
heart for gastronomic
satisfaction There is
selection in species
for some little ones
grow firm Others put
to rest at heart's suggestion
perhaps request
Palm oil of dark tropic
seat overshadowed by
wine which cleans insides
Offered like tea in
agrarian spots a
touch tingles body
which dances with memory
of their trees challenged
by provoking storms
Svelte squirrels collect seeds
cupboards of snacks for
little ones to store
Small buttons swept or
Piled into heaps they
propagate disintegrate
Give green birth feed trees

Intention
In isolated places
discreet garden paths
or land forgotten
of a violent past
Palms look up pleading
flexible fingers
on venerable hands

Smoke green grey shies
away from company
of trees A lifelong
need to gather energy
silently work as
others do clean redistribute
collectibles of weighted
wandering air

Living Space

Braided cover of little
trunks home to creatures
tiny tough Palms are
condos from fronds to
roots Majestic grey
trunks give fungi a
start While at tips birds
cacophonous chatter
before roosting for
routine tomorrow
Arguing for space unleash
dissipation on
unknowing patrons
of parks Palms' sheltered
sphere tenants must pay

trespassers will be
showered with palm flowers
multitudes of seeds fertile
white grey brown waste

Challenges

Tall palms with fronds of
a kind The dying
points downwards hugs trunks
then dries Watch out in
wind storms Fronds fly fall
from unhampered skies
New area exposed
middle growth continues
trees grow taller new
muscle is seen by
craning necks at base
of root ridden tree
Headless skeletons haunt
fields walks gardens when
fronds wave down lightning
on its race to ground
Diseases will come
sympathy waved if
drought heat wave or cold
return to its place
Bent character of reedy
form suffered injuries
survived storms Soil is
vast there's choice Many
content to avert a
fast Seed will choose to
suit the state tree craves
Cousins siblings not

all are alike some
fronds like tines of inverted
fork impales itself
on blue winds called skies
bending straightening
obstinate to forces
that could alter fate
cause yield snap break

Festive Trees

Beneficiaries of trees
are gratefully pleased with
myriads of services
supplied by graceful
palm trees Nights dark cold
or hot decorative shapes
perk people up Revellers
are drawn to lights like
moths but trees need rest
like all of us How
can it be if hundreds
of needle like bulbs
pierce fateful energy
into skin of trees
Years of healing sets
itself right System
will weaken efforts
in vain Majesty calls
to cut bands of heat
perpetual light
from desiccated bark
Festive folk will find
their way out in warm
clear or cloudy dark

Harmony

Will resistant blades
of noble dry fronds
tie the knot between
palms and persons Celebrate
new age of compliance
thought growth change
with exquisite alliance

DECIDUOUS

Trees are upset
from lack of sleep
The pricking of lights
at Christmas time
into barks on leaves
of non-evergreen trees
irritates bio-rhythm
of sensitive beings
Juggling temperatures
in equal space time
weakens constitution
invites disease Then
begins a process
elimination of trees

RENEWED AGAIN

Earth repairs
with
explosive bouts
of feverish coals
with
fainting spells
from stressed torn joints
with
futile flames that
clear mountains plains
with
spotted sickness
that saps vital liquids
with
alarming chemicals
that inhibits birth

New species emerge
in lovely concord
with revised systems
Earth strengthens first
then changes route

REVIVAL

Every morning day

evening night regard

demise of some light

Bulbs burn out--our Sun

flows brown then plunges

wearily pass backgrounds

Raindrops darken stars

play light Sun has screen

of optical delights

All hit the earth then

bounces back to feed

on dancing darkness' fight

with flickering flames

of expanding light

SOUND BANK

Hollow drums disperses
sound Sonic journey
through insouciant worlds
Plethora of waves past
deepest caves Rock clay
sand gobbles tones that
hisses around for
eons to return in
measured time to old
spaces filled with promise
whispers ready to be
heard Slivers of soft
sonorous sounds float out
of slight cacophonous mounds

SUMMER SAFEGUARDED

Light of expiring
sun so fierce--pierces
unconcerned air Plummets
through an orange red
then faint atmosphere
Muted at night floats
on life Air swells little
altered in this summer's
casual morning to
morning continuous
light Burnished cap on
pink subtle bright

SYNERGY

Fabulous designs

faces for wine rubies

bluebells cinnamon songs

Hands for giving stroking

saving Feet for exploring

dancing visiting dear

ones Skin that shelters

machinery functioning

as one

A RIVER'S TALE

Rio Cobra's cupboards
are sinkholes-floors quicksand
It curls along lazily
in foreign areas of
same land - Green water
spiced with minerals mud
feeds on limestone - carves
digests in hundreds
of years bits pieces
not nearly missed -
detected by scientist
peering into a glass dish

A pelting deluge
river comes down- panics
tears at corners pours
out of trough - frantic it
dashes for reluctant
ground-Invincible bridge
of iron and stone-
recipient of messages
from floods roaring down
on helpless friends - No
one thinks river hides
mines in muddy beds

Water uncovers bricks
of bullion deliberately
lost four centuries before
by hiding inhabitants

fleeing pirate shores
The River remained
to protect its store
A child with a stick
poking scraping found
proffered gold beyond
imagination - she looked for
a rainbow No reflecting
colours on cloudy sky
No story of hidden
treasure - no one knows

River how much we
see you offering food
treasures challenges to
land with small fee - For
interest is lasting
a surprise reassures
River has geography
to protect stores from
fears - corroborate with
children of coming years.

CONCLUDE THAT

Earth survives
Aquatic kingdom changes
course - all will leave
Charted plan takes weather
pollutants man and
motley entourage
through fog- unfold mysteries
in obstinate mines
See through cracks to objects
below covered by pitch
Yellow sun explodes
a golden brown reflects
fresh sparks from a cold
deep dark past - Rio Cobra
snaking your way
through a deep gorge
hiding under mountain
hollows clawing at clay
avoiding sunrise or
cloudy days - now the change
Ground is white perforated hard
Limestone cloistering mysteries
in the darkest cupboards
of a Merman's home.

Aldyth M Irvine-Harrison

TORTWISTER *

Feeds on warm cold air

gushes out to freedom's

call Bellows of approach

is clear Where to hide

a flash dive fear No

time Darkness simplifies

goals Go within without

is closed Rip roars tears

rakes Picks up trees hurls

them back Decapitates

homes snatches contents

menaces subterranean

moles Pirouettes up

with graceful swirls

throws balls of ice dust

melting hail Amid litter

glittering crystals

small relief to areas

smashed and cold with grief

*Neologism

UP MOUNTAIN LANES

Brown grey rocks sprouting
pale purple ochre orchids
Deep green trees under
a tropic blue that
surrounds buildings roads
Winds freewill in shady
pools of mineral springs
Mountain stretches to pawn
its peaks to atmosphere
warm discreet Random
streaks of golden light
illuminate strings of
plants wisps of flowers
resting beside tumbling
waters feeding on mud
minerals lulled by humming
of tepid trade winds

Adventure seeking gain
from snowy covered
rocks of screaming heights
A shudder of growing
bulk enfolds intruder
Great grandparents often
need rest do not welcome
streams of continuous guests
Some conquer peaks they
stake claims Mountain allows
a sweet moment to visit
see their garden of

snow ice neighbours below
with stark grey rocks--then
GO before gates creak
crunch bang snap lock
Mountains groan shake grow
honour cries for needs
not desires Excesses are
beyond gates of wisdom
of enlightened states
Species of deer cats
sheep goats rodents birds
diverse residents received
their permits eons ago
to roam cold heights
colour temperate zones
Indeed sequestered Snowy
Leopard climbs into secret
cave night after night
Stomach sweeps rock frozen
ground Luxuriant white
under specs of brown that
warms vacant spaces
hunger's home Perseverance
involves double strength
to transport family meals
up high without implements

Mountains breathe sigh sing
as part of each living
thing They deplore fouled
fresh air treatment of
their inhabitants as
game depleting stores
poisoning rain Alternatives
cry out to be employed

spare animals plants human
kind Winter's dark lit
green red orange colours
shifting squeaking seeking
electrical replies
White peaks perch on bumpy
terrain Polar hats
on cracking moving mass
Mountains melt on solid
nights will reappear with
staunch blue white moonlight

WORD

Word a cataclysmic

roar or a twinge of hope

that sets up the motion

from within Evening's orange hope

night's silver yearning

Dark absolves the light

on things Light dissipates

the night within

Animal Kind

HOUSE HUNTING

Scanning summer garden

we noticed with dread

that our quiet tenant

had fled Beautiful

boys in black and white

scampered underneath the

deck Teasing night air

with designer smells

that quelled activity

for that night's little sphere

They must be shopping

for a new abode

Scattering of naphta

balls will play historic

role in sending this

second family to seek

a more inviting home

LEOPARD SEAL

Foraging loner
last to leave southern
ice Feed upon skinny
forms of dying birds
fleeing seals fish in
hiding You scrape for meals

MOONLIT MORNING

Pre dawn at kitchen window
peeping at garden's
snow Caught moonlight reflected
in icicles that clung
walking from upper floor
Traced shadows of maple trees
that criss-crossed entire
acre's core Abandoned
darkness under portals
of wooden carved doors

Wonder what's it that
worried a skunk pungent
odour labelled me drunk
Tail pointed high--claws
dug into crater's shadow
drawn by platinum moon
Silver black camouflaged
in this morning's afternoon

POLAR PLIGHT

White mass black tongue nose
lumbering lightly on
with padded feet Dark
claws will dig grasp meal
Splotches of red on
white Tale of hungry
family's fight Hold on
gasping food needs to
breathe cannot remain
beneath robust ice
untenanted green sea

RETURN

Former pet scratches
wood Smells footsteps where
corners fret closed door
space available Pet
runs right in Rancid smell
like wet stored boots Food
in plate by kitchen door
Grief evaporates Joy
implores Emaciated love
eats bathes rests relives
Joy loves re-inhabits
empty vacant place

TRAPPED

A field mouse slid under
grill of enclosed patio
There were snacks drinks
no crumbs on stone floor
A pair of large eyes
saw mouse screamed Hurried
to hardware store Remedy
inexpensive simple
no fumes no crunching
trap just double glue
on white paper mat

Two mornings later
a splendid day with
aquamarine skies
breezes running chasing
leaves in tireless fray

Shriek shattered wavy
wind Tiny animal glued
to page It looked up
blinked captured hearts Vet
was called how to free
sweet thing by wet bar
Pool cleaner knew right
antidote for paste
released gentle blinker
to far away green
high grassy place

Human Kind

AUNT CYNTHIA

Aunt Cynthia do you
remember a cheeky
tobacco plant rooted
in a safe corner
between terrazzo steps
and a light coloured
wall of your house--home
for birthday parties
cakes ice-cream sandwiches
lemonade Spontaneous
Christmases dancing
playing Some childhood
irritants kept some
little people in bed
Screams sniggers swished by windows
playing hide 'n' seek
capture the base
On the telephone you said
your brother's wife had died
I must go for the
Children--they have lost
their mother you cried
The family now larger
the plant grew fat leaves
fed by sun rain contentment
in budding environment
far relation to the
smelly short straw on lips
of adults puffing clouds
at the nosiness of

their curious young kind
Was it bothersome when
we wormed our way out
of milk without syrup
then bribed the dogs with
vegetables we spurned nor
knew But stop recall
such dancing dancing
dancing Uncle Bill and you
At ninety nine you
told a little fib
said you were sweet sixteen
with twinkle and grin
Your face had a glow
no wrinkles or spots
gave hints to other times
your loving lot relatives
friends sliding away
from time-filled earthly stay

One hundred and one
short a few weeks you
remained serene Love
you gave you received
again and again
from loving caregivers
A ring of amorous light
lifted your comely spirit
away out of hearing
from our earthly sight

FORMER CUBAN CITIZEN

Yesterday Uncle Paquito

took the flight of each

lifetime--he flew on

wings of joy earned from

a lifetime of service and

painful Cuban memories

His map pure light that

glowed like satin ribbon

on a stark black velvet path

Yesterday a devoted

professor befriended

a clear space--filled it

with green memories

danced away from the

mundane invoking a

sheltering mist of relief

Yesterday Uncle Paquito rested

Cleansed of impurities

he lay with breezes

whispering to the

sheer curtain behind his

single bed It was

then he completed

an earthly leg of

the journey that would

unite him with souls

he cherished and held

Yesterday we said

Hasta la vista Uncle Paquito

Hasta la vista

WE

We -some of the people
Will call some of the shots
We must silence opposition
inappropriate or not
We must ridicule strike fear
Approbation - pay no heed
We are bullies of invention
Through Arts of Connections

We some of the people
have been sanctioned to silence
Must regard little tears
In soft vests undeclared
Must shudder at the noises
Infecting our serenity
Will grieve at the loss of
Compassion and Dignity

We all of the people
Have never found the Graces
to enhance all races
At places in our midst
questionable weeds abound
to sweeten or poison
Our International Grounds.

INTERMISSION

Late evening children
small Fathers watch over
sleeping stalls of mischievous
minds chubby hands faces
dreaming summer stunts
Mothers walk blue moon full
free play in mixed fruit
on popsicle sticks
Kick off shoes swing in
parks Laugh off routines
that fill August in part

Exchange news that slid
beneath newscasters
eyes regulated lips
Laughter high saunter
along Avoid untamed
crossing still avenues
Sleep descending like
clouds over a mist
Path winds onto a
garden's peace Light dark
lawn traced by crocheting
trees Corporeal webs of
blue white lace purchases
time in our sleeping space

KIND APPARITION

Dreamt of Peter late
teenage protector
in vivid shirt of
weekend colours Engineer
at core leaned on a
frame of an unfinished
door Stuffed a lifetime
of nature's designs
to fit an environment
he never resigned
Then hands shook he could
not draw or type Explained
but speaking shrivelled
Now rays of colour
fit his smile--he waved
receded faded
in bright fog-like flakes
of blue snow at morning's
end of a night's late
television show

THE OTHER SON

Illness misgivings
pills substances took
him to vague worlds neither
dark light knowing nor kind
A hollow filled with
smoke of comforting
cigarettes Body crammed
with hamburgers starchy
foods brief television
songs Beer refreshed form
that could not sing or
talk indeed of things
Uh huhed* response gave
no clue to faltering
understanding or
intelligence renewed
He called his mother
placed blame on her
head for seeming lack
of love praise food after
many forgotten wakes**

Comfort to her soul
was three minute dialogue
Glimmer of hope afloat
in sultry dark fog
clawing at light flashes
She passed with memories
of glowing shiny
spaces--left dark love

of a son to dry
*Sound of agreement
** In some cultures a vigil. It is a celebration with much
food and drink some days after a death or a funeral.

PRESERVER

He shouldered a family
name not unknown Mother
served in her area well
Father died with concern
for a son--felt obligation

to this proud lonely head
A gardener of rare thought
practice care respected
life everything everywhere
Embraced talked with animals
no meow whimper fear
Guarded his passion
for plants bushes trees
Uproot those weeds they
take over the lawn
See their flowers fruits
his indignant reply

He made odd seats with
pieces of wood from
dignified dead trees
that dried in the sun
Evenings he melted
at the feet of trees
to smoke his somewhat
sacred weed Perhaps
to contemplate for
his closest contact
it would seem were trees

Some die softly--ragged
beauty lay bare when
they rip themselves in
kamikaze flay
For trees may uproot
with thundering roar
keel over dry roots
hauled from their nesting
chambers in brown dry
leached ground Trees decide
his boneless reply
He died in the night
at a hospice and
like the trees that dried
away inside cancer
ate slowly he slipped
silently into
a brand new drive

SIDEWALK OBSERVER

Vote--talk into air on
walls recall what was
done unsung compromised
There is wisdom in
flakes of paint on posters
past their prime indeed
Up ahead scandals
like balls rolled on track
as hopefuls take final lap

Champions presumptive
shackled to old years
State could resettle
for four more years
So issues pocketed
environment cries as
memory leaves cage--questions
why many forgot they
were frozen with charm
eager with forgiveness
then the 'X' was installed

IF I DIE WHILE DANCING

If I die while dancing
don't make a fuss screaming
Stay! Stay! you're deserting
us - Crank up the music so
I'll hear as this spirit
of life floats on through Worlds
of atmosphere - the melodies
must continue matched to
so many strains Don't distort
the rhythm you too enjoyed
Dance on let feet explore
light sound music in -outdoors

If I die while playing
discordant notes - rolling
into harmony yet unheard
Hold on to that strain-let
it lighten the heart
don't think about performer
who must let it resonate
Feel notes eternal with
other universal sounds

Passings are new beginnings
bright openings into an
infinite pool that inspires
our creation How do
we create - Why can't we
reap a fistful of air
from a wide open field

WIDOW'S WEDDING

She wished to be married
again Kind to elderly
grieved for the sick A
small item which no one
spoke--she loved everyone
that entered the house

Obliging security
guard followed tradition
hugged neighbourhood in
motorcycle arms
Housekeeper riveted
slid into the care
of soldier-like bulwark
against harm despair

A wedding suggested
all agreed a kind
caregiver recognized
on the street Dress rented
bouquet readymade
food wine paid for by
quiet collective plate
Best man arrived on
a powerful machine
shook up the flowers
watered preened for a
ceremony under trees

Highlight of wedding
when stories unfold
lovely lines on her
generosity--appeal bold
"Don't look at the face"
gasp then snickers when
amiable bride threw head
back abandoned arms
roared with a laughter
that unsettled guests
Some raced to bathrooms
or held fast their chests

Political correctness
little ground where
directness is inbred
with good nature not scorn
This was no insult
there was no gaff-- a
forthright citizen spoke
all agreed--focus
on face is fruitless
feel a heart be pleased
for what we perceive
leads to contentment
or invites disease

MOVEMENT

PROLOGUE
Statistical studies of our human populations,
Followed the races from emergence through migrations.
The tendency of people on mass to new banks,
To be viewed as a menace embracing foreign camps.
Demographers studied and recorded the passages
Of mass migrations throughout human ages.
Homogenous groups were easy to track
As they hiked and flew to luscious spots.
Now, there are favoured communities on this sphere,
Wherein lies a magnet extracting from the air
Multitudes of persons, diverse in customs and wear.

AN IMMIGRATION OFFICER THINKS
Do humans have a monopoly on the potion
To keep our appendages in perpetual motion?
We make many journeys in our life's vacation,
To visit or flee or explore new locations.
The flight through the womb is the life adventure,
The Immigration counter is studded with tension.
Numerous features pleading arrogant or pleasing,
Colours from ebony to brown gold and fleecing.
Have they no questions? What are they seeking?
Work, matrimony, peace, snow or yearly heating?
How many souls have I dispensed with today?
What will my Government have at length to say
If I allow in too many or too few, or give stay
To one linked to the other political plea,

Will security be risked on the back of a flea?
A thousand questions gallop through this mind,
A hundred I need ask to justify to my kind,
That I executed my duty, right on the line.

OBSERVER
Political doctrine poured into the young,
Balloons and grows then festers the tongue.
Quite inconsequential what side you are on.
Doctrinaire uttering tears heat from the sun,
Smothering in the folds of some toothless gums,
It chases out citizens and ultimately, attracts none.
MOVEMENT

THE REFUGEE SPEAKS
We travelled out swiftly on a moonless night
So no one could explore the depths of our fright.
Horrors behind us, anticipation we would wrestle,
In the rickety bowels of a fisherman's vessel.
The nights were many and the days so few,
Then the heavens silvered to alarm us anew.
The paradox of moonlight brilliant and bare,
Illuminated the waters, made them quite clear
To our probing destiny. Darkness seemed nigh
The moonlight had severed lights from our sky.
Mankind of devious thoughts and manners,
Squander the designs of the greatest of planners.
Not all would survive, some made it ashore
On a lush island we thought civilized and pure.
A scandalized press recorded our history,
Dispassionate faces investigated our mystery.
An alarmed public viewed us with such curiosity,
As we set out to construct a struggling community.

TO KIN

Some may be lonely without family attachments,
Umbilical cords if stretched to the limit,
Will tear, detach and cut off from the relative.
Loneliness makes a low muffled drone,
It hopes that the echo will create a loud moan.
Loneliness our creation or an original sin
To depress and motivate the movement of kin.

FOR WORSE

Characters do not always flee injustice,
Or seek employment with greater remuneration.
There are those who have stolen or committed treason,
To seek sanctuary from laws was their only reason
For bolting their country, not revealing where,
And pleading persecution or the agony of fear.
Some still believe, still others hold dear,
No extradition treaty with our country this year.

MOVEMENT

PAST ATTACHMENTS

A man and family of a far eastern land,
Thought of his plot of land all winter long
The family he forfeited, the place of his birth,
Hi new bride is beautiful and perfectly borne.
Familiarity sustains us to each novel morn.
One will not find the old country the same,
New ones impetuous or perhaps lame.
The vibrations mutated but the features remain
Like sentinels, scrutinizing a long altered plain.
Humans do not walk backwards; it is not their design,
Even when we think it seems right at the time.
The movement of people back and forth,
Will colour the complexion of some uniform port.

CHRONICLE

Pockets and stomachs new organs of the brain,
With capacity for hunger the source of pain.
Craving's a condition that inflicts all nations,
From earliest time to our present generation.
In the Fifteenth Century, first Portugal then Spain
Went searching for spices, others played the game.
Countries were claimed, they CRIED OUT for owners,
Like orphans marching towards new borders.
These places were fruitful, their soils crammed with gold,
And silver and copper and precious stones.
Or the earth mothered plants, cuddled their roots,
Which yielded crops to become an essential food.
How we hurried through the ages until now,
To find new places with a bountiful store.
The indigenous peoples died or were integrated,
Some embezzled from homes and borne to new faces,
They nourished the appetites of the powerful in high places.

MOVEMENT

HUNGER

Luminous eyes and distended inclination,
More than craving to scald the imagination.
Fettered feet are towed through shelled sands,
A vision of skeletons with anomalous glands.
The ceiling bright blue and the floor empty yellow,
No stalk would seek solace in dust red and mellow.
Clouds had once gathered, exploded and fell,
Rain failed to make inches in a bottomless well.
How slack mouths gaped to gather the drops,
Which trickled down pipes evaporated and stopped
To sizzle like steam, in the alimentary canals
Of ancient desert children. The shadow of the hungry,
Ominous and divorced from green greed,
Had set feet in motion with survival its creed.

FONT OF FAMINE

We did not think to leave our village,
No one had suffered the terrors of pillage.
Our children played through the ages on farms,
Of millet and nuts and mutton and corn.
Clouds of locusts had roamed the air
Decimating the green with voracious flair.
The skies rumbled black, blue then white,
Then split its sides in an iniquitous fight.
Its liquid poured forth to drown the earth,
We drained, revived and replanted a store.
When nature slaps man and man fights back,
No one is victorious, both regroup and re-attack.
We hack at our trees and cheat the elements
Of an ally on earth to release its rainy pelts.
And the bubbling sun in all its glory,
Pours out gold rays that are hot and hoary.
The greenery succumbs and sends messages to man,
To evacuate his beloved ancestral land.
On dust laden paths, feet bleeding and bare,
Too hollow to wonder, new strangeness will appear.
A horrified world get wind of our plight,
Old help was half-hearted, it's a political right
To instigate an exodus and exhibit our might.
Two decades beyond, once seated at last,
The new generation may never experience a fast,
Nor think outside oblivion to take to tasks,
The invisible agents of their destinies in decorative masks.

MOVEMENT

INHERENT MOVEMENT

The trees is stationary but roots travel far,
Through rocks and sands, silt and war.
It's the legs of the tree where travel is sure,

The toes puncture steps and break open the door
Wherein lies adventure, and food and wealth,
In the form of seeds that litter the steps.
Swept of the vegetable kingdom do as they ought.
Survival of the species their one intent,
We see this from the way plants are bent
Away from the wind, hot sun and driving rain,
In a passionate struggle to protect the family name.
So even the herbs will endeavour to migrate,
Within the regions that their constitution can take.
Heed many animals in their classic migration,
In search of food and away from conflagration.
Their reasons not infrequently similar to man's.
Crying out for sustenance and for the land;
Never stationary, never caught tight,
In an iron gip that tears at delight.

EPILOGUE
The swirl of our movements in tune with this planet,
Mirrors our sun with hot gases in orbit.
When craving is over and famine is stilled,
Man's curiousness launches new tugs at the will.
New frontiers are pulling at the inquisitive thread,
That throughout ages unraveled us out of our beds.
Humankind will have dashed around the globe,
Mixing a sweet batter of all peoples
In the bowl of the earth. With finger-like ripples
That billow and stretch beyond the earth's lines,
Migration of all races to space in our times.
1,375 Words

ABOUT THE AUTHOR

Aldyth Irvine Harrison was born in Kingston, Jamaica, where she received her secondary education at St Hugh's High School for girls. She studied at Concordia (Sir George Williams) and McGill universities. She taught many levels in the Quebec school system.

It was her choir master, the late Brian Brice, and fellow chorister Dr. Thouria Bensaoula, who encouraged her to publish *Patches in & out Two Centuries* which was published in October 2010 by Éditions du Mécène, Beauceville, Quebec.

Her concerns are about the careless handling of our Earth. The dignity of the Earth's environment must be nurtured, respected and preserved. She enjoys telling stories and travelling to different parts of the world.

She resides in Montreal, Quebec, with her husband Robert and family.